Food for Thought

Food for Thought

Top 7 Tips to Improve Your Health

GEORGE S. COOK

Copyright ©

Copyright © 2019 George S. Cook in partnership with The Vitality Guru

All rights reserved. No part of this publication may be reproduced, distributed, or transmitted in any form or by any means, including photocopying, recording, or other electronic or mechanical methods, without the prior written permission of the publisher, except in the case of brief quotations embodied in critical reviews and certain other noncommercial uses permitted by copyright law. For permission requests, e-mail the publisher, with subject "Attention: Permissions Coordinator," at the e-mail address below.

publishing@thevitalityguru.co.uk

Ordering Information:
Special discounts are available for print copy versions on bulk quantity purchases. Please contact the publisher via the e-mail address above, with subject "Attention: Bulk Sales Request".

Printed and written in the United Kingdom.

Revised Edition

Dedicated to a close friend, and family associates that inspired me to take action and to offer support along the entire journey and to have allowed to make this all happen.

Preface

This book has been written for the sole purpose of guiding and offering knowledge to those interested in changing their diets. It is to my understanding that the human body's sole purpose of eating is to offer it the ability to function at an optimal level.

Through extensive research and experience with human anatomy, food chemistry and the biochemical reactions that take place within the body from what is ingested, the following statement was observed; that ingestion into the body of any substance is directly linked to how the organs and all other parts of the body function for a subsequent period of time post-ingestion. From this, the take away from that what we eat and consume into the body plays possibly the most crucial role in affecting how not just how our bodies function, but the state of their physical and mental health as well.

It was after this I decided to get accredited into the field of Nutritional Therapy, to back up my understanding and knowledge within the field and to offer a sense of trust with the information I would otherwise be offering unaccredited.

For many now, the approach to caring and knowing about one's personal health state is an ever-growing movement. With more and more people than ever becoming conscious of their health, we're seeing mass declines in the consumption of poorly produced products including meat, hydrogenated oils, confectionary, dairy and many other forms of food ridden with synthctic products, chemicals and toxic substances. The initial movement for many was the rise of Veganism in January 2018, and with the movement growing and expanding, more and more people are asking more and more questions concerning the food they've been purchasing and what exactly it includes.

I have written this book for all those who are deciding to take interest in their health and food. Although I talk highly about the benefits and superiority of veganism when it comes to personal health, the information I've provided can be used and incorporated by anyone to improve their nutrition levels, approach to eating and possibly to the state of their overall health.

Contents

INTRODUCTION 1

WHAT IS A VEGAN DIET? 3

SALT 9

SWEET TREATS..15

EAT WHOLE / ORGANIC 22

GOOD FATS..32

PROCESSED FOODS...................................40

DARK LEAFY GREENS 45

SUPERFOODS...50

A REASON WHY 55

7-DAY CHALLENGE 67

LAST WORDS..72

INTRODUCTION

Although it shouldn't, what I'm about to tell you often comes to a bit of a shock to many who aren't prepared for it. The secret to feeling well, to living a happy lifestyle full of energy, well-being and vitality is at the source of what we fuel our bodies with; food. There's a huge reason anyone who's taken part in improving their nutrition will happily sit you down and appear to lecture on the amazing benefits is that you simply cannot refrain from wanting all those you love to experience them also.

As a nutritional therapist in study, and someone who has done a lot of research into food, plant-based nutrition as well as the biological effects on the human anatomy that specific produce can have, whether on the brain, heart and other vital organs or the body itself as a whole, I can happily promise that eating a diet full of nutrition and eliminating the consumption of toxins will bring your body back to a state of health you probably couldn't dream of.

It is with that in mind that I have composed an array of different actions an individual can take as a step to improve one's diet if they require ways to do so, either by increasing their nutritional levels or by removing harmful substances.

The following approaches are advice on how to improve your diet, and hopefully, correlating to an improvement in one's health and well-being. I make no claims as to what can be promised to be achieved following the advice, as it varies dramatically from person to person. I can, however, offer you that this information has been well researched and analysed to provide you with an understanding to as well as an array of ways to help you take control of what you're putting in your body, so in turn, your body reaches a state you want to be in.

WHAT IS A VEGAN DIET?

Since we first entered 2018, veganism (the lifestyle and ways of living vegan) absolutely skyrocketed. Prior to this time, too many people, it was seen as nothing more than a ridiculous and melodramatic hippy trend that many believed was just a load of nonsense. Not many people realise but the term and way of living 'Vegan' have been about since 1944 where members of the Vegetarian Society decided some of their newsletter to be devoted to non-dairy vegetarianism.

We now have top supermarket chains all around the world endorsing whole ranges of 'free from' foods, whether that be free from milk, gluten, wheat, egg or soy, whatever you wish to avoid in your diet, there are options available. There is almost nothing you can't buy straight from the supermarket, meat-free bacon? Got it. Dairy-free milk, yoghurt, cream and protein shakes? Sorted. Gluten-free pasta, bread, cakes, etc.? They have that too.

For me, Veganism or at first, eating a plant-based diet changed my life. It changed who I was, my focus and mental abilities, my fitness levels, my organ and body health, my weight, my moods, my social circle and even how I acted with those whom I knew. It changed me and I could not be happier with every branch of result that came alongside the change.

Eating any free from or health-conscious diet has never, and I repeat **never** been easier than it is today. With all of the media highlights, growing supermarket stocks and masses of animal rights activists making the public aware of the true horrors that go on behind the curtain of many food industries, we are seeing more people than ever interested in vegan and strict vegetarian lifestyles.

The term 'vegan' is the idea of living a life in a way that is as sustainable as one can be with the utmost respect for the planet that has blessed us all with everything we have and will ever have. That means living in a way that you do what you can not to take from another part of the planet that we cannot sustain, as well as to avoid harming or causing suffering to any other animal or human or the planet as far as possible for an individual's own desires.

This includes not consuming any animal products such as meat, eggs, dairy or any other animal-derived produce where ever you can, avoiding the purchase of a product that was unethically created via the exploitation of another human, animal or in any other way harmful to the planet or environment whether from production to consumption.

For many people, this seems like an impossible task. However, anyone that suddenly suggests you break up with lifelong habits is going to lead you to that feeling, however, it is so much of a simpler, smoother and more rewarding process than most of us could have ever imagined.

Veganism for most is much more than just a diet but a philosophy and way of life. We do not seek pride in our ways but we wish to share with everyone the true benefits. Whether that means the almost constant elongated elevation of mood, the superior energy levels, the beaming energy of vitality we receive or the fact we accidentally treated, reversed or even cured some forms of disease or disorder within our body we thought was not possible, or maybe even something we never even knew was causing us suffering until it was alleviated.

If you don't start a vegan diet on the basis of helping out animals, most usually do so to help their personal health. No matter what your original reason, these become rather prominent very quickly. Vegans themselves have naturally become health conscious (aware of their state of health). In fact, from the vegans, I've spoken to and the trainers and clients I've also met, I can honestly say most vegans are more health aware than even some of the most extreme dieters and athletes.

The most common and obvious trait is the elimination of meat and dairy products, which any vegan can instantly tell you why. Despite what many of us grew up to believe regarding what goes on within the industry, these food sources are no longer packed with high-quality proteins, minerals or other nutrients we require. Not only are the products completely lacking most of their nutrients, but the same product is created in such poor and cruel conditions, pumped with chemicals and hormones and exploited beyond possible belief of the many.

The second, of course, is eating a whole load of (or rather, only) plant products. You don't need to be a vegan, or even a vegetarian to know that fruits, veggies, nuts, seeds and whole grains are amazing for your health and that lots of sugary treats, fizzy drinks, cakes and fatty foods such as takeaways are ruinous and detrimental to your health and wellbeing.

After these two factors, the rest is pretty much up to the individual. We are not angels, we are not perfect and we slip up. Some of us choose just these two factors and that's more than okay, in fact, that's superb! Everyone's lifestyle, dietary requirements, financial status and many other factors dictate how 'strict' they can be with their nutrition and lifestyle.

In this book, I am going to be sharing with you the most helpful and easiest tricks that you can implement into your diet to improve your nutrition and make your vegan (or non-vegan!) diet replenish and promote vibrant health throughout your whole body!

SALT
LOWER YOUR SODIUM INTAKE

Table salt (aka. Sodium chloride), although often regarded as a necessity to your health and as a substance categorised as a mineral (but one that much more closely represents a drug, an artificial, and extremely harmful toxin to the body), is being consumed in shocking quantities, much higher than even the recommended daily upper limits suggest. Due to this, salt has since become one of the major causes of both heart disease and stroke around the world and is responsible for around two and a half million deaths globally per year!

We should be consuming around 1,500 – 2,500mg (1.5 – 2.5 grams) of natural, organic salt per day. The UK average for table (refined) salt is well around 8,000 mg (8 grams). That's between 3 and 5 times the daily recommended levels! The average intake for vegans and vegetarians, unfortunately, isn't much lower either, around 6,500mg daily—which is still way too high.

Why is this exactly? Well, most statistics will tell you it's due to the high consumption of processed foods worldwide, around 70% of all the salt we consume is already in the foods we buy. I suppose that means if we didn't consume these foods, we wouldn't have a sodium issue, and that may be true. However we have neglected salt as a vital nutrient and mineral and adopted it as almost a prime ingredient into anything we make, we have become so dulled down to its superior ability to enhance almost any flavour that we have to pile loads more on to receive the same effect and unfortunately this comes with very negative health effects.

The most well understood (but completely ignored) effect is its effects on raising blood pressure. High blood pressure is the leading cause of cardiovascular disease, it accounts for around two thirds or all strokes and for around 50% of all cases of heart disease. However many people believe that other than making one feel dehydrated, its effects stop there. They don't.

The excess sodium we consume ends up in our bloodstream and the kidneys have a very hard time trying to filter it out. Through repeat overindulgence, the sodium accumulates and the body holds on to as much water as it can to try and dilute the increasingly growing levels. This causes an increase in both the amount of fluid surrounding your cells as well as the volume of blood cells in the bloodstream. This increase in the volume of both blood and water within the bloodstream means more work for the heart as well as more pressure on the blood vessels – hence why it's likely to lead to heart attacks and high blood pressure.

Over time, this will cause the blood vessels to stiffen, making the body even more susceptible to high blood pressure, heart attacks and as well, strokes. Also to add, where the build-up takes place in the kidneys, production of kidney stones are also rather likely. High sodium intake has also been shown to damage the heart muscle itself, the aorta and the kidneys before it is shown to cause a rise in blood pressure.

When our body excretes salt – often through urine, it also takes along with it another very vital and important nutrient and mineral; calcium. With calcium being one of the many 'trigger words' for a vegan (a word or phrase that sparks a strong emotional and often personal involvement), it should definitely be something you're already aware of however to many, this fact remains hidden.

For those with a high sodium intake, when it comes to excreting such via urination, the body takes calcium with it due to their close regulatory connection within the anatomy of the body. This brings about two major issues; high levels of calcium within the urine which is well understood to lead to the development of kidney stones and as well, the leftover low levels of calcium within the body leads to the onset of osteoporosis (brittle bones).

So all in all, we can clearly see the astonishing and detrimental effects a high sodium intake.

Constituting to over two million global deaths each year, two-thirds of all circumstances of strokes and around half of all cases of heart attacks. If that's not enough, remember that repeated high consumption is a sure fire way to cause the development of kidney stones, the weakening of bones and a way to make sure the body's vital organs struggle more and more until failure.

All bad aside, remember that natural, organic salt is still a vital nutrient just like any other vitamin and mineral, in fact, salts like Himalayan pink salt contains all 84 of the bodies required minerals where table salt is one of the deadliest foods you can consume when repeatedly consumed in high amounts. Aim to keep within the range of 1,500mg and 2,500mg daily depending on your caloric intake. If your sodium intake happens to be over, aim to drink a little more water for that day, as salt and water work together in the body to keep a homeostatic balance. But don't forget to bring the intake back down a bit, otherwise increased consumption of both only causes additional stress to the heart.

Additional Note: Potassium (found abundantly in dried fruit and adzuki beans) is another vital nutrient and mineral to the body that actually brings on the complete opposite effects of sodium, although it cannot be used as an arguable supplement to continuing a high sodium diet, high potassium intake can actually help relax the blood vessels, lower blood pressure and help excrete the unwanted levels of sodium. In fact, you should make it your goal to always, yes always consume more potassium than sodium every day (around 4,500mg potassium and 2,000mg sodium).

SWEET TREATS
REFINED TOXINS

To those reading this who are already following a vegan or vegetarian diet, I shouldn't really need to remind you of the negative effects sugar has or can have on your health. In fact to anyone, either following or not following any specific diet, sugar, especially highly refined versions, should seriously be eradicated, whether for it's extremely poor (essentially empty) nutritious profile, it's damaging effects on the body or it's highly addictive properties, white refined sugar is one of the worst food products man has created and sold. Period.

The white crystals in your sugar bowl have been extracted from sugarcane via a fairly long process- involving machines that crush the plant to squeeze all the juice out. That juice is then filtered and boiled down to remove the moisture, then that product is refined through a number of chemical and mechanical processed to finally end up with what we know as the crystalline, white refined sugar, which also contains no protein, no fat, no fibre, no water, no vitamins, no minerals and no enzymes.

To throw some comparison into perspective as for the damage sugar can have, sugary fizzy drinks alone (yes, just-drinks) kill twice as many people every year on average than that of the illegal drug heroin, and four times that of cocaine in the US alone, four times! Now don't get me wrong, of course, sugar is much more readily available sugar to the world than these illicit drugs, and of course these drugs are much more harmful to an individual but for such a common ingredient and additive in our food, it's rather shocking to see such a high mortality rate and that's not even the reason I used the world toxin in the title, but we'll get to that a bit later.

Do yourself a quick web search on how many people are killed by the effects of sugary drinks each year and you'll see its way up into 6 digit numbers, 180,000+ deaths per year to be specific which is absolutely appalling. Remember, this also doesn't include any of the confectionary, chocolate, cakes and other goods people consume with high amounts of sugar, let alone the pure refined sugar we all have huge bags of in our kitchen cupboards.

On top of this, let us not forget to mention all the serious damage sugar will do to your health along the way to causing an early death if you're not careful. Of course, the first is weight gain, and possibly the unhealthiest weight gain your body will ever endure, receiving no nutrients, spiking blood sugar levels at an alarming rate and wiring a very fast addiction through your mind is just the beginning.

The most common disease from sugar consumption is type 2 diabetes, a disease where consumption of white refined sugar in high amounts quite literally 'breaks' the body's ability to digest glucose (the base molecule in all forms of sugar). Yes, white refined sugar will actually cause your body to not be able to process sugar at all unless you want to be taking repeat prescription injections of insulin because your body couldn't cope with it in previous forms and quantities.

You're also at a very high risk of developing heart disease, high blood pressure, stroke, gallbladder and liver diseases, osteoarthritis, fertility problems in both men and women, respiratory problems, sleep apnoea as well as colon, breast and endometrial cancers. The list goes on.

However even with this understanding, due to sugars extremely addictive properties, many will struggle to just say no. Even whilst writing this, I was tempted to chuck some into my coffee despite having many sugar alternatives available in my home. Without addiction being a factor, most would whatever sources they had and bin them almost immediately, just as anything seen as an immediate danger to oneself and loved ones is instinctively dealt with for the safety of those involved.

Just like a drinker can state the negative effects of alcohol, or a smoker can tell you not to ever pick up your first cigarette and any other form of substance addict could shamefully tell you how they're not proud of themselves, next time you buy something high in sugar, you'll be aware of these facts and either consciously make the decision not to buy, or notice how instantly your mind is programmed to go for it.

Continuing on with sugars negative health effects, we haven't even mentioned the more commonly known but ignored effects on high sugar consumption; the damage towards dental health. So we all know sugar rots the teeth which if you aren't aware, is because it becomes a food source for oral bacteria, yes you're not only eating the sugar, the bacteria that rot your teeth will live on it too. Mix this with the body's warm temperature and the moisturised environment of the mouth, lo and beyond, a breeding ground for bacteria is created.

Refined sugar is also highly acidic, giving it the ability to strip off the protective enamel and decalcify the mineral structure of your teeth. Sugar also helps to prevent the proper flow of oral fluids; which primary purpose is to fight forms of infections and bacteria in both the mouth and the body.

Now to answer the question why I referred to sugar in the title as a toxin, that's simply because even in the most minuscule amounts it will do more harm than it will good. In fact, baring the easing of your craving, there is no good effect of white refined sugar.

White refined sugar is often referred to as an 'anti-nutrient', due to the fact it actually has to take nutrients from the body to be digested. Vitamin B_1, B_3, C and calcium the most, but also require trace amounts of magnesium, potassium, zinc, sodium and chromium in order to absorb and use the caloric energy within the sugar molecule.

Considering most of the population are living on diets lacking many proper nutrients alone, just imagine the damage high sugar diets are doing to these people. Remember, the primary purpose of consuming food is for supplying the body with these nutrients, or trace chemicals so it can function optimally. Sugar, essentially being a poison is not only straight up harming the body in a whole range of ways, but it's slowly stripping you of so many vital nutrients also.

As a final note, I will point out up until this point, the word sugar is predominantly regarding white refined sugar. However, it is vital you stay away from consuming high amounts of any highly refined or processed form of sugar, including high fructose corn syrup (glucose-fructose syrup), table/caster/icing sugar, glucose, dextrose, maltodextrin, maltose and of course fruit juices.

Don't get me wrong, you don't have to go 'cold turkey' and never consume anything sweet ever again after reading this, that's not what I mean. Just be wary. Be conscious. Have the self-love to look at what you're about to put into your body and just be aware of what it's going to do. There are so many beneficial natural sweeteners, natural sources of sugar and delicious foods out there that you don't need to subject yourself to the more harmful foods we see marketed anymore.

EAT WHOLE / ORGANIC
FOOD IS FOR NUTRITION

Food consumption is for nutrition, not for pleasure. It likely seems I'm advising you to eat the most boring, bland food sources I can find, trust me I'm not. However, this is a vital fact of survival that we've all seem to have forgotten. We may have evolved to make very tasty forms of food whether nutritious or not, but we cannot ignore the purpose of such a vital necessity for our survival unless we want to be very unhealthy of course. I imagine if you're reading this, then you likely have some want to be healthy, especially as you continue to read on.

Back on topic, food consumption serves two basic requirements for our body, providing nutrition and energy. The 'small stuff' really matters when it comes to nutrition, which is what's categorised as micronutrients. It includes vitamins, minerals, antioxidants and phytochemicals (plant-based nutrients), and are the minute but very powerful amounts of chemicals we find in foods that make up all the chemicals our body requires to function at full capacity. Then there are your macronutrients. These control your energy levels (calories) and often take up three main categories of fats, carbohydrates and protein.

The majority of people conscious of their health, unfortunately, mistake micronutrients to be less important due to the word micro as the prefix. This is not the case. The term micro in this sense is regarding the minute amounts of substances we require, however without sufficient vitamins, minerals and antioxidants, not only can your body not function anywhere near optimally and can eventually lead to death, but these micronutrients are responsible for performing all of the bodily functions to process the energy from what you eat.

I advise you to eat both whole foods and organic, simply because they're really the only food sources where we can get adequate nutrients. All other forms of processed, mass produced and 'artificial' forms of food contain partial to likely zero nutrients.

So what are whole foods? Whole foods refer to the unrefined counterparts of many staple dietary choices of today. The main culprits being whole grain pasta, wholegrain / whole-wheat bread, brown rice, quinoa, barley, buckwheat etc as opposed to the refined, white versions such as white pasta, white bread and white rice. The refined forms of these foods are not only much higher/denser in calories (which is not what most of us want), but they have also been completely stripped of their nutrition, leaving nothing more than empty calorie fillers.

The benefits of swapping out refined foods for whole sources include reduced risk of the following; stroke, type 2 diabetes, heart disease, inflammation, colorectal cancer as well as they greatly help to support weight maintenance.

As for consumption of foods that are organic, the term refers to the ways that agricultural products are grown and processed. They are essentially the naturally created foods we have always consumed up until recently, where foods are being modified and played with to manipulate taste, colour, size, nutrition levels and longevity. All for the sole purpose of corporate profit.

Regulations vary from country to country, however, the common ground for organic produce is that the crops must be grown without using the following; synthetic pesticides, bioengineered genetics (GMOs), petroleum-based fertilisers and any sewage-based fertilisers. I really don't want to put people off their food but it seems crueller for this to remain secret.

I understand that organic produce doesn't last as long, is harder to come by and is often more expensive for the buyer. In all due respect, it's not been made easy for us to come by organic produce in the past few decades. However, in regards to the price, less of the product will provide more benefits. For example an organic apple will be possibly upwards towards double of that of a non-organic one, however, the nutritional profile will serve much more to the body than two of the non-organic apples tallying up at the same, or a higher price. I want those who read to decide for themselves what they would rather have, so here's a detailed unbiased analysis of each component used in non-organic produce.

Synthetic pesticides are used to increase the yield of a plant crop more so than organic pesticides and they come in numerous classes, however since the 1930's we've seen evidence of these pesticides having quite adverse effects on the reproductive, nervous, endocrine, immune and central nervous systems within the body, as well as other effects on the environment. Not to even mention some of the ingredients being found in these products such as glyphosate which was proven to be linked to a major list of birth defects.

Bioengineering genetics or genetically modifying organisms is nothing new. It's a process that's been used widely in the last few decades as a means to provide cheaper, and larger quantities of produce from both plants and animals. Although from a business perspective this seems quite a good idea, we are still yet to see the long-term health affects consumption will have on the population's health.

The main problem is that these foods lack nutrients, so even our fruits, vegetables and animal products are seriously lacking in quality. They may contain nutrients on paper, but nutrition is so much more than vitamins and minerals once you learn to understand how the body works. Simply put, whatever you ingest, your body takes from.

A fully organic, naturally grown plant that has learnt to adapt and survive in a tough environment, will bring you a lot of nutrients, compounds like fibre and phytochemicals that are produced naturally by the plant to help it survive against harsh weather conditions, predators or pathogens. We then ingest these high-quality nutrients, phytochemicals and compounds that offer our body the ability to do the same as the plant.

Eating a genetically modified and low nutrient dense organism will inherit the body with not only a lack of nutrition, but a lack of vital microchemicals such as phytochemicals as well as contents like fibre and minerals etc., depending on how the organism was modified. In essence, you can see these foods are merely there to keep you just about alive and breathing, in fact, they keep you so far from obtaining health and vitality it's unreal. Quite literally, your body is of what you eat, eat genetic modification and it's likely you'll end up developing a genetic mutation (in medical terms, this is referred to as cancer growth), eat an organically grown plant with powerful phytochemicals and create a body that can naturally protect itself from all sorts of disease, damage and infection.

Petroleum-based fertilisers (or any fertiliser for that matter) is used to place nutrients into the ground once a crop has been harvested. Synthetic or petroleum fertilisers are used in corporate harvest for a magnitude of reasons. The main being they are extremely cheap, they can be specifically altered to have the exact ratios you require for your crops and they work much faster, meaning as soon as you harvest one crop, you can plant the next and it will almost start growing instantaneously.

The problems being with the fact these fertilisers are synthetic. Rather than be found naturally, with high levels of nutrients and that which is naturally created and properly bound on a chemical level, synthetic fertilisers are extracted from the Earth in a way that is rather damaging to the environment. Organic fertilisers, on the other hand, are made naturally from plant and animal waste (compost and manure) or powdered down minerals.

Petroleum is an oil. It's obtained from crude oil, which is what the massive oil pumps out in the ocean are extracting constantly. The dangers of this, firstly come from that it is a finite source as far as we are aware, or at least it takes longer to produce than we're using it. This is the same oil that is used for all oil-based fuels.

The petroleum is also highly processed and refined, which like with any form of oil, really disrupts the chemical structure and can make the difference between a vital nutrient and a highly carcinogenic source of energy (raw olive oil in comparison to repeatedly heat-treated olive oil for example). These fertilisers also do not help promote the health of the soil, they just increase the yield of the plant.

And lastly, the use of petroleum has a negative impact on Earth's biosphere also, damaging ecosystems through events such as oil spills and releasing a range of pollutants into the air including ground-level ozone and sulphur dioxide from sulphur impurities in fossil fuels. The burning of fossil fuels is also believed to play a major role in the current episode of global warming.

In essence, the once organic, healthy plants are now growing synthetically with a lack of nutrition from the soil, and a nice amount of likely carcinogenic petroleum fuelling its growth to help that of the yield and bring about more money, quicker and easier.

Finally, the fourth factor for produce to be regarded as organic is that it's free from sewage-based fertilisers. I've already explained what fertilisers are and how they work, do you really want them being grown in sewage waste? Naturally occurring manure from a healthy animal that eats nothing but organic grass is rather different to the mixture of human faeces built up from chemical ridden foods, meats, sugars and whatever else the nation is consuming. I can promise you now it doesn't even compare to manure, even if they are both waste products. I definitely don't have to go into any more detail here.

So unless you consciously now wish to be consuming products that either lack vital nutrition to keep your body functioning optimally, it's highly advised you make the swap to whole food sources. Luckily these are often not only cheaper surprisingly depending on the produce, but they are actually must tastier than their refined, bland counterparts.

As for swapping to organic produce, this is understandably a little trickier. Food is more expensive, it doesn't last as long and is harder to come by. Remember this is about improving your diet, not instantaneously 'fixing' it. My advice is to make the changes wherever you can.

To begin with, I recommend you either consume the most nutrient dense foods in your diet as organic, or you swap out the foods you consume in the highest of quantity for their organically sourced versions. This way you will have the most effect on your health and nutrition in one lump sum, then the rest you can tweak as it becomes appropriate. Depending on what you eat and where you live, the cost of either method will vary dramatically, however, neither should be too pricey, in fact, for their health benefits, the price is highly efficient.

GOOD FATS
THE TRUTH ON FATS

Fats, for many people, seems to be a horrific word to use in dietary terms. For decades now there has been an endless stigma surrounding one of the vital groups in food consumption. Fats have been used as a marketing tool by so many different companies to sell you all sorts of 'health' based products it's almost unbelievable.

Due to the name, many have taken upon the assumption that fats are bad and make you overweight. This has also given rise to a whole range of low-fat food products being sold to those with an interest in losing weight, despite them not always being too healthy for the consumer. Like any category of food, we have products that are extremely poor and even toxic to our health, we have products that are low or empty in nutrients and then we have high-quality sources containing full nutrient profiles.

There are also many different specifications of fats, there are saturated, polyunsaturated, monounsaturated as well as partially hydrogenated (trans-) fats. You've also got essential fatty acids like omega-3 and omega-6. You can continue to break the categories up further and further, however, that's only going to add to the confusion.

Before we start, not all fats are created equal. Many of the sources in the modern diet, unfortunately, live in the lower, unhealthier end of the spectrum as well. In fact, most modern diets are plagued with all forms of unhealthy fats, hence the major rise in cases of poor heart health coming by in younger and younger generations.

The instant rule is that any source of fat will be healthier if it's been cold pressed, rather than being heat pressed or treated. This is due to the fact the heating process causes the molecules to change chemically and actually become rancid, which is essentially a term synonymous with cancer-causing within the body. Rancid fats are oxidising molecules or oxidants. This is what anti-oxidants are working against, hence they're seen as a defence against cancer growth.

The second rule is price. If it's cheap, it's cheap for a reason. Fatty foods are not cheap. Avocado's, nuts, seeds, nut butters, coconut, they're all high priced foods. You're not going to get an abundance of these foods squished and pressed to get a small amount of fat that's going to be sold for a fraction of the price of the source, that couldn't work. Remember, just because it's a vegetable oil, it doesn't mean its fine.

Go to your supermarket and look at all the cheapest oils and fats, canola, sunflower, rapeseed etc. There's a reason they're so cheap, mainly because they about 90% if not more, created by genetically modified (GMO) ingredients, but I'll get into this a little bit later.

First of all, get partially hydrogenated or trans-fats out of the picture. These fats are repeatedly heated and come as a by-product of saturating unsaturated oils. They hold zero nutrition and the fat molecules are essentially 'mutated' under literal definition and have been highly linked to cases of cancer and have been found to be highly carcinogenic.

After decades of saturated fat being hated, the medical community was shocked when a 2010 study in the *American Journal of Clinical Nutrition*. In a research analysis, scientists discovered that there was not nearly enough evidence to link saturated fat to either heart disease or stroke.

Saturated fats are found mostly in animal products such as milk, butter, eggs, meat and cheese but in plant sources such as coconut oil, coconut butter and flax seed. Any fat or oil that is naturally solid at room temperature. Science has shown us that the consumption of saturated fat in animals is unhealthy and bad for your heart. This is due to the fact there are no nutrients contained, or very little with higher quality sources.

Many people are already well aware of the health benefits of saturated plant fats such as coconut oil or flax seed, this is due to the fact that these contain high amounts of essential fatty acids, as well as a properly formed nutrition profile – the opposite of the mutated chemical bonds found in trans- (and other heat treated) fats. In fact, these forms of saturated fats are converted to the much more heart-healthy monounsaturated fat once inside the body.

Then there's unsaturated fats, mono- and poly-. Scientifically, saturated fats are 'saturated' in hydrogen, monounsaturated is one hydrogen molecule from being saturated and polyunsaturated is more than one hydrogen molecule away. It is this minute chemical difference that makes a whole range of difference to the overall product.

Monounsaturated fats are found in nuts, seeds, avocado and extra virgin olive oil. This fat has been proven to raise the body's good cholesterol levels and has been linked to lower risk of stroke and heart disease. This type of fat is recommended to be consumed daily and to make up the majority of your daily fat intake, although I highly recommend you eat a variety of these sources, rather than focusing solely on one primarily.

Polyunsaturated fats are found in walnuts and walnut oil, flax seeds, canola oil and most other seeds and nuts also. In fact, there is no singular food that contains just one category of fat, they all vary in different ratios. Like monounsaturated fats, these have also been shown to be healthy for the body, there is still a bit of misunderstanding on the high amounts of consumption however polyunsaturated fats like omega-3 have been proved to decrease the risk of certain cancers. Polyunsaturated fat is an essential part of the diet as it cannot be produced in the body, however, it isn't necessary to be consumed every day.

To summarise everything, consuming fats in this order from highest to lowest is where the uttermost benefits can be taken from each, but remember cold pressed sources over heat-pressed or repeatedly treated sources always. Monounsaturated fats such as nuts, seeds and avocado, saturated fats such as coconut oil and flax seed due to their chemical synthesis within the body making them into monounsaturated fats also. And lastly, polyunsaturated fats like walnuts and canola oil should be consumed, however not as much as monounsaturated fats as they are not as 'essential' to the body and need not be consumed in as high of amount every day. This also allows us to make sure we aren't consuming too much of these as we are still unsure of the effects of high consumption.

With a varied consumption of different fat sources, rather than one shutting out vital nutrient categories of food due to fear of becoming overweight or having a heart attack, we actually open the doors to a whole range of health benefits we've avoided due to repetitive nutrient deficiency.

Not many people realise or wish to accept that fats contain a whole range of very important and vital nutrition that can have an astonishing effect on our overall health. In fact, an entire subsection of vitamins (fat-soluble vitamins) literally requires us to eat sources of fat within our diets to transport their nutrients into and throughout the body, instantly rendering a low and no fat diet completely deficient in nutrition due to the lack of certain consumptions.

On top of that, essential fatty acids like omega-3 and omega-6 are vital to be consumed for body and brain health, due to the fact they cannot be synthesised within the body but also that omega-3s actually consist to around approximately 8% of the weight of your brain. Not only are they a source of protection against the heart and brain, but they have an immense ability to optimising the many facets of brain function, from depression and mental health to your cognition and memory as well. Recent research has also revealed the understanding that omega-3s have profound strengths in the ability to half age-related decline and pathology, destroying the long-believed medical belief that brain shrinkage and nerve cell death was progressive and irreversible.

Lastly, many of these healthier sources of fats (excluding essential fatty acids) actually have been proven and shown to have many positive effects on your heart and blood health as well as decrease the risk of developing cancer. This has been proven in many scientific studies and tests related to how a lot of the healthier fat sources harbour the ability to raise your good cholesterol levels.

PROCESSED FOODS
UNDERSTANDING THE PROCESS

When I say processed foods, I am referring to foods that have been highly or repeatedly processed and often mixed with an alarming blend of artificial or synthetic products or chemicals. Anything baring a whole, organic food source (for example a beetroot) is classed as processed unless the product was straight from nature and sold in its natural form.

Not only is it highly impractical both from a health approach as well as a lifestyle approach and maybe almost impossible for many to completely negate any form of processed foods, it's also highly unnecessary.

In regards to what to avoid, I want to make it very clear that I mean highly and repeatedly processed foods. That means something that was taken and put through many different chemical processes and reactions, blended with chemicals and combined with all sorts of taste enhancers and in return became part of a product that no longer resembles the original source.

An obvious example is raw cacao beans being created into chocolate bars. After undergoing 8 different processes, the bean becomes a rather healthy equivalent of the modern day equivalents. Add in the fact that many confectionary companies of today mix blends of milk, lactose or whey powder into the mix, as well as a tonne of sugar, E-numbers and high polyunsaturated vegetable fats, we're receiving a product that contains almost nothing of the original source, other than a minute fraction of some remains.

In small amounts, the original dark chocolate bar included within the example can actually be rather beneficial to one's health, which shows how processed foods aren't necessarily bad, although even at this stage, a vast majority of the health benefits and nutrition to the original cacao bean. Once processed further, blended with synthetic chemicals (E-numbers), mixed with lots of sugar, low-quality milk powders as well as rather unhealthy blends of fats, the question of why we're consuming the product begins to come into place.

The answer, as the majority of people give is that we simply enjoy it. The food has been scientifically analysed and created to be as stimulating to the taste buds as possible, through the use of sugar and flavour enhancers; which are highly addictive substances.

Of course, this goes far beyond just confectionary. Everything from meats and dairy products, to tinned produce and dried goods as well as drinks and alcohol. The thing to look out for is how cheap the product is. The more highly processed, usually the cheaper the product (think tinned spam vs a grass-fed steak or cheap margarine vs raw extra virgin olive oil etc.).

Another rule is nutrition labels. Food standard agencies require a product's label to state what is included, both via a list of ingredients as well as nutrition label. Take a quick read, are there chemicals or ingredients you've never heard of before? And is there any additional nutritional information such as vitamin levels or fat profiles? If not, then it's pretty fair to say the product contains no nutrition.

Although the processes involved will vary from product to product, the usual basis is often along the lines but not specifically just subject to the following. Repeated heat treatment at high temperature, killing off any good or bad bacteria as well as destroying a lot of the nutrients and other important chemicals. Stripping off any fibrous outer layers (think shells and husks) where a lot of the products immune fighting and defence chemicals are situated. Blending with other highly processed substances as well as the addition to many synthetic or artificial ingredients used for flavour enhancing, increasing addictive quantities or 'forcing' a product to maintain a structure that isn't chemically natural (plant oils into solid, highly processed saturated fats).

The body itself is also not designed to accept these unnatural compounds. Being just as much of nature's creation as anything else, we are designed to strive organically. Foods that go through rigorous and repeat processes become foreign to the body, they are unnatural. The body doesn't know exactly what to do with the substances, so they are poorly utilised and often can be even quite harmful. It is, for this reason, it's advised to limit, and aim to consume a diet that is low in terms of overall processing as possible.

DARK LEAFY GREENS
NATURES HIDDEN MIRACLES

Dark leafy greens are a powerhouse of nutrients. They are truly the most overlooked but yet most beneficial source of nutrition to the body you can find naturally. This all comes down to the concept of nutrient density and the foods that are the most nutrient dense.

It is important to understand what empty calorie foods are as well. Empty calorie foods refer to any form of product that contains a really small amount of nutrients that our bodies need to function in comparison to the overall quantity. Meaning that the empty calories we consume are not useful for our bodies.

The nutrient-dense food, however, is the opposite. Foods that contain very high amounts of vital nutrients for our body in comparison to the quantity. This is not only beneficial to our bodies in the fact we are consuming the vital nourishment it needs to thrive but due to the density of nutrients, we don't need to consume piles and piles of the stuff.

Some of the most nutrient-dense foods, amongst hemp seeds, parsley and raspberries are dark leafy greens. Darky leafy greens are also extremely, and practically non-existent in terms of calories. A single swish chard leaf contains 100% of your daily Vitamin A requirements, and 3x the requirements for Vitamin K, all alongside only 9 calories! It is also right at the bottom at number 9 of the top 10 most nutrient leafy greens per calorie.

Dark leafy greens are not only great sources of Vitamins like A, C and K, but they are packed full of many other nutrients we ignore. These greens are packed full of minerals that are essential for our bones, teeth, hair and muscles etc, antioxidants that give the ability to fight off oxidising carcinogens and powerful phytochemicals, which are chemicals found specifically in plants that are created to help the plants defend from damage from pests, weather and harsh sun rays etc. and it's well understood that consumption of these foods in our diet nourish our body with the abilities to do the same.

Many struggle with the consumption because they're unaware of how to prepare or to eat leafy greens, we've all been so well conditioned to just throw a bowl of leaves together and call it a salad, that we've forgotten the thousands of other uses and ways to flavour not only our greens but other plant-based produce as well. A little search across the internet for recipes, vegan or not, can definitely throw some ideas, but in all honestly, they are extremely versatile.

Many leafy greens have a very neutral taste, so can be added into many dishes easily. Others, such as kale carry a bit of a more bitter taste, so more seasoning would likely be helpful, however, due to the nutrient density of these foods as just discussed, we don't have to go out of our way to choke down piles and piles of plain leaves.

A handful of kale or spinach added to a smoothie is more than enough, a handful of spinach or cabbage added to a stir fry along with some other veggies, filling up wraps with a mixture of your favourite etc., they're extremely versatile. They also disintegrate down to almost nothing once cooked so if you're trying to sneak a bit more in, try them in your cooking. Even easier, get a mixture of greens and boil them down into a stock, broth or soup and use them in any of your favourite dishes for a base packed full of not just vitamins, but minerals, antioxidants and phytochemicals as well, all at the price of almost no extra calories whatsoever.

It's no wonder Popeye was well known for eating his spinach. Despite popular belief in the health industry today, meat is not the perfect source of muscle growth. It may be an option, but it's nowhere near ideal. Although muscle growth does require adequate calories more than anything, from a blend of fats, proteins and carbs, it is the vital micronutrients that allow the body to not only produce more muscle, but it allows the body to undergo many essential parts of the process, including the breaking down of food into energy, which is one of the main functions of the b vitamins complex.

Without these micronutrients, the body is simply consuming, partly digesting, and emitting high amounts of vital micro and macronutrients within your waste products. This is why despite popular belief, most vegans maintain, or even gain additional muscle when swapping their diet, despite likely drastically lowering their calorie and protein intakes. Simply the body functions much more efficiently, so less is required but more is still received.

This is, in fact, one of my main advocates when discussing a vegan diet with people who still choose to eat meat and or dairy. Most realise this soon after making the change, that once swapping out for plant-based produce full of nourishment, the body thrives so much better in every way. Your energy levels, your mental clarity and focus, your mood and the overall ease your body has partaking usual activities is greatly heightened, showing us how much more efficient the body becomes in a range of ways.

SUPERFOODS
NATURES POWERFUL MEDICINES

If there's one thing that ranks top of the list of most nourishing and nutrient dense foods, its superfoods, as the name no doubt suggests. Superfoods are essentially foods that contain astonishingly high levels of nutrients in comparison to the quantity of the source. They're very compact sources of nutrients.

For reasons medical research has still yet to discover, some of these superfoods have absolutely unprecedented positive effects on the body. Simply put, it makes a lot of sense. The human body, like the rest of the world, is designed for a specific and perfect way by nature, just like every other being. To strive, all it requires is nature.

Many have forgotten this and reached out to synthetic and artificial products to try and reach a healthier, natural state. It just will not happen. It is our body's true nature to be at a pinnacle of our own health daily, to be full of life and energy to do whatever tasks we wish to accomplish.

Far too many people in today's world are reaching out to highly processed foods, protein powders, artificial vitamins and synthetic chemical drugs to be healthy. It makes no sense. A car is designed to run off an oil-based fuel, if you started feeding it a substance completely foreign, that had negative effects on the inside pipes and parts, it wouldn't perform at its best. The body works the same way.

Superfoods, along with herbs, spices and a few other things are natures superior and healthier alternative to medicine. They are substances that can be taken in microscopic amounts that provide the body with the chemicals it needs to detoxify itself of heavy metals, prevent things like cancer growth, drastically lowering blood pressure, cholesterol and chances of stroke as well as helping to promote weight loss, increase energy levels and more.

The above goes for a product known as spirulina. Spirulina is a blue-green alga, a freshwater plant that is one of the most rapidly growing superfoods today. It's so highly packed full of nutrients that even the World Health Organization calls it a 'superfood'. Although not the most pleasant to the tongue, small amounts go a long way towards helping your body fight off disease and supporting a healthy, vitalising life.

Other superfoods such as chlorella (another algae very similar to spirulina), which in fact comes from the same family are very high in chemicals that are often not even considered by many in the field of nutrition. Such as phytochemicals, phytonutrients. They serve various different functions within plants, helping to protect the plant's vitality. Luckily for us, they also provide benefits to those who enjoy eating them. That's because they have health-promoting properties including antioxidant, anti-inflammatory, and liver-health-promoting abilities just to name a few.

Another great superfood is Nutritional Yeast, often called yeast flakes. It is basically just dried inactive yeast that comes with a sort of nutty, parmesan taste. It works great in any savoury dish as a vegan cheese flavouring alternative, and even better it comes absolutely packed full of vitamins.

So packed in fact, that just one serving of 5 grams contains more than your total daily B_1, B_3, B_5, B_6 and Folic Acid. As well as 88% of your B_{12} for versions that have been fortified, 64% of your B_2, as well as an awesome amount of Biotin and Zinc.

And it's essentially just vegan cheese powder. That means it works great in any dish that would accompany cheese from spaghettis and pasta bakes to burgers and pizzas. And it's a superfood!

The great part about superfoods like these is you can make even the most 'junkiest' of foods super packed full of health-promoting nutrients. Even half a pizza can contain over 60% of all your daily total vitamins with the help of superfoods such as yeast flakes, plus you'll love the taste.

Healthy eating, and more importantly, eating for vitality doesn't need to be boring, plain or dull. Thrive to eat the most colourful, dynamic, flavoursome meals packed full of nutrients and you'll wonder why you ever ate any worse, to begin with.

A REASON WHY
WHAT'S SO GREAT ABOUT A VEGAN DIET ANYWAY?

One question I truly get asked above all else, about the way I eat, whether because I choose a vegan orientated diet and lifestyle or because I choose to spend a much higher amount of money on my food than most people I know is "Why?". Why on do I choose to appear to *'limit'* myself so much with what I can eat and why do I choose more expensive versions of foods that could be purchased for a fraction of the price?

The truth? I don't. I don't limit myself with anything. If I want it, I have it. That's the idea of living free isn't it? Having whatever you desire? It's that I've looked into what's in these foods and I've negated all want for them. Yes, I would adore the taste of a velvet chocolate fudge cake with vanilla ice-cream, just as I did every time I ever ate out, ever.

However what I don't desire is the intake of high amounts of refined sugar that are going to strip my body of the nutrition I've obtained for the day that my body needs. Nor do I desire the blend of low quality and highly processed, genetically modified rapeseed and palm oils used in the cake also. I most certainly do not want to go near a frozen whipped up blend of sugar and a cow's bodily fluids we have force pumped out of her whilst blending it with God-knows what else. Yes I'm well aware of how that product would appear to my tastebuds, but unless someone was to offer me a version that is beneficial to my health or at the very least neutral and has no real effect, then why would I want it?

My most simple and blunt answer I can give to why I appear to be 'strict' on myself in comparison to others is that I care about my body. That's not really true when most people, as long as they keep clean, brush their teeth, don't eat takeout every night, do some form of physical movement in the week etc. all care about their body. If they didn't then their actions would be very different from the ways that they are. However, I believe it is that we don't care about our bodies enough.

I don't believe I'm even that strict on myself, in fact as I continue this journey I aim to get stricter and stricture until I am able to consume absolutely what I desire the way I used to desire the fudge cake, but my desire leaves me full of nutrients, antioxidants, phytochemicals, minerals, water, fibre and all the rest. My aim is to eat in a way that promotes my body with the ability to fight off all disease and illness, without ever missing out on something I want.

Over time our standards have dropped for what we consider healthy. We're convinced that eating food riddled with all sorts of unwanted additives that are really bad for the mind and the body and not doing much more than walking a bit each day is what we regard as healthy, or at least the norm and vegans, fitness advocates and those who've looked into nutrition are seen as extreme, fanatical and strange. Granted if strange means away from the norm then that last point is accurate.

Where we've accepted this as the norm, everyone's decided to live there thinking it's alright, that there neither caring nor not caring for their health, they're just living a fairly normal, average life. In reality, these people don't realise that they're subjecting themselves every day to harmful chemicals and tonnes of other unwanted things that are slowly causing their body to disintegrate and their mind to become more and more imbalanced. In fact, vegan or not if any of the above tips are something you could use to implement into your diet then there's likely something that you're consuming in the way of that which is still rather harmful.

Where most people fail to realise they're actually doing harm is because the damage is minuscule bits at a time. At first, you may just read that and be asking if there's even any point in eating better if the damage is so minute, however, the damage is the only minute when in really small amounts.

If over the course of a year you had subjected yourself to consuming a couple of packets of biscuits, no you won't see any negative effects on your health. One because you're not consuming enough but also because your body is fed so well aside from that it can fight anything that's consumed which it doesn't agree on, in essence, you'll probably just need to go to the bathroom upon trying to digest it to allow your body to kick it straight back out.

However when we subject ourselves to this kind of foods daily, and by these kinda I do truly refer to anything that is not a natural, whole, plant-based product although I respect it's much easier said than done, your body is going to be overloaded with all sorts of chemical cocktails that it's not sure how to deal with, many of which begin to cause physical deterioration of the body but also, where you've also not fuelled your body with the necessary products to fight off these harmful substances, they are left to take full control over the health of your body and of your mind.

This is what I meant at the beginning of the section where I stated I care about my body, my health and my mind etc. The word care is a little shallow because my ways to many would be extreme, over-care, however, I still don't think I'm there yet, I still have improvements to make also.

I believe to the truest extent that you really are what you eat. And no I don't mean you'll become an apple if you eat 4 apples every day or you'll be looking like a chocolate bar if you consume them all the time but at the end of the day, it is only food and water (at least it should be) that we are allowing to be consumed into our bodies. That being that if it wasn't for what we ate and drank, we would become very sick and perish within just a matter of days.

So we really are what we eat, if we eat nothing then we cease to exist in life at all. Also realise though, that our only consumption other than water is food. The food we consume is the entirety of what fuels our body. The main reason I stopped eating meat and dairy is that I realised that these animals are dying in severe torturous conditions, being mistreated and live very sick lives of high stress right up until they bleed out. I don't want to see that on my plate, I sure as hell don't want to consume the literal remains of an unconscious, stressful, abused, sentient being that's muscles are soaked in stress hormones, poor nutrition and synthetic additives that made it grow unnaturally large or quick.

What makes plants, or at least organic whole plants so much better is that not only are they not subjected to any of that, which should really be more than enough of a reason but on top of that, on top of also containing an abundance of vitamins, minerals and antioxidants literally designed by nature to be the perfect sources for our body to get what it needs but you're also consuming other, smaller substances like phytochemicals. Chemicals that the plant had used to adapt and survive against weather conditions, predators, pests etc. These phytochemicals which have been designed to keep the plant alive at all cost, are now being absorbed into your body and you inherit the power of whatever you eat.

That's what is meant by you are what you eat. If you consumed a plant that gave you super strength, well after consuming it you would become super strong. You literally inherit the ability of what you consume. The choice is yours, stress hormones from meat, synthetic petroleum pesticides and genetic mutations from low-quality plant foods or powerful, defensive phytochemicals designed by nature to keep something alive above all else.

You are what you eat, but you'll also eat what you are, your self-image is going to be a major factor in how you eat. If you want to know what you think of yourself, look at what you eat, it'll give you a massive push in the right direction of finding out your self-image, your levels of self-respect and how much you value yourself.

I'll be honest with you, I was the worst person for eating vegetables and all things healthy. I had no idea how the heck I was meant to survive to be a vegan, I actually expected myself to get very skinny and poorly. In true honesty, on the day I switched vegan I had only ever eaten a carrot, cabbage, swede, leeks and parsnips because that was what was given to me as a child and teenager when my mother would cook a roast dinner. I had never cooked my own vegetables, let alone eaten them. I didn't eat nuts, I didn't like beans, I'd never eaten leafy greens, none of it. I would pull the peppers off my pizza, the lettuce from my burgers, even the onion and chopped tomatoes from my pasta sauce. I was worse than most 5-year olds.

To no surprise now when I look back, I was living a very miserable, unhappy life where sickness and disease were constantly reoccurring. In fact, it was so prominent, there was a time in my late teenage years where something else came up before I had fully healed from the last issue I was dealing with.

I couldn't get my head around it before, I was so sure I ate healthy (considering I was eating what is considered a 'clean' diet of mainly chicken breast, eggs, milk, rice, pasta etc.) and working out properly 4-5 times a week as well as doing a lot of cardio. On paper I was living like an athlete, however, on record, I was heading to the hospital.

So don't think that because of how I speak about food now, how much of an advocate I've become that I've had it any different than you, that I was born into a home that offered me lush organic foods from a young age because it didn't. My grandmother grew up as a livestock farmers, I spent my teenage years growing up on a farm and my dad was a chef who ate more meat than I could have sworn was ever good for even carnivores.

In fact, I'm the only one in my house that eats plant-based, or even close to 'healthy' by the standard I listed above. From the very start, I had to learn what to buy, how to cook it, what to make and then how on earth I was supposed to eat this weird plate of food from the day I made the change. I didn't have any support, I had willpower.

For me though, veganism wasn't enough. It was the step I needed to take to finally push my diet in the right direction but I wanted more. Someone asked me a couple of years ago, they said if I had a Ferrari or any sports car for that matter, would I use fish and chip oil as fuel.

Of course, I said no, looked at them with a face that probably seemed a bit lost and confused, but also portrayed that they're asking a really stupid question. However, their reply stopped me in my tracks. "Well if you wouldn't fuel your Ferrari, why do you fuel your body? If you can afford a Ferrari you can afford to fix it if you can't then your life is still great without it, however your body, you don't get another chance with it, you can't buy a new one or fix it once it's ruined."

Not only did this make me realise how much that as a society we all care about material items (and most people will tell you I am very non-materialistic), but how little we care about our bodies. How little we cherish such an invaluable, brilliant, powerful gift we all received at birth. How little we even notice what we already have.

So if like me you wouldn't chuck a load of dirty oil in your awesome new sports car, then what on Earth are you doing with your body, with an even more expensive, powerful, tremendous version far greater than any Ferrari could ever be that you never get to replace. You wouldn't throw a load of sugar in the petrol hatch, you wouldn't pour a can of fizzy drink in there either. You would likely cherish it and make sure it receives the best fuel you could afford. So why don't you?

Why are you pouring fizzy drinks into your own supercar that drives you through life? Why are you consuming harmful substances that you now know are going to slowly rot the insides away until it no longer runs? Unlike the Ferrari, realise that when your engine goes, you don't just step out and call your insurance to fix it all, realise that when that moment comes, your moment comes.

I can't make you want to eat better, I can't make you want to feel better, that's going to have to be up to you. I can tell you what to do, I can share with you why I or others choose to do it but at the end of the day the choice is up to you, if it wasn't I'd have already changed your nutrition for you so that you wouldn't have to try but unfortunately that's not how things work.

7-DAY CHALLENGE

It is to my belief that this wouldn't be an effective self-help book if you couldn't finish it off with a plan of action to take with you. You may read the information, you may research some of it but if you don't really have any plan for you to follow from today then nothing's going to change, you'll forget by tomorrow and continue as you are, having just completed reading another book on your shelf or device. With that, I have to offer you the 7-Day challenge.

The challenge is simple, for each day of the week you're going to implement one of the above tips into your diet. Each day, you're going to add one more, until finally at the end of the week you're living a single day where you're literally 'living by the book' as far as this book is concerned. Vegan or not, I want you to experience the benefits of eating healthier.

For example, your week should look something like this:

Day 1: Consciously **consume less salt** – you can do this by eating lower amounts of high salt foods or adding less salt to your meals and even better, replace it with salt that's great for your health like organic Himalayan pink rock salt or Hawaiian lava salt etc.

Day 2: Consume less salt and **less sugar** - you can do this by eating less confectionary, biscuits etc or by using a sugar alternative in your hot drinks.

Day 3: Consume less salt, sugar whilst **swapping out GMO** products for **organic** and **swapping bleached, processed grains** for **whole counterparts.**

Day 4: Consume less salt, sugar, swap out GMO and bleached, processed carbs and **increase intake of good fats** – simply swap other oils for a raw, organic coconut oil or consume a single avocado.

Day 5: Consume less salt, sugar, swap out GMO and bleached, processed carbs, increase intake of good fats and **remove any other processed foods** from your consumption – food should look like the source it resembles more now, you should be eating primarily ingredients that you're creating meals out of yourself.

Day 6: Consume less salt, sugar, swap out GMO and bleached, processed carbs, increase intake of good fats, remove any other processed foods from your consumption and **get a load of dark leafy greens in your diet** – a soup, smoothie or salad is just the beginning, if you want to look online and be adventurous, do so!

Day 7: Consume less salt, sugar, swap out GMO and bleached, processed carbs, increase intake of good fats, remove any other processed foods from your consumption, get a load of dark leafy greens in your diet and finally, **find and purchase a superfood** that you think you might enjoy – if you like cheese, nutritional yeast is similar to parmesan, if you like naturally bland, go for macadamia nuts, if you like greens, try out spirulina. If none of these takes your pick then eat a punnet of organic, fresh berries, they're packed with all sorts of goodness for your body.

After the seventh day, congratulations on completing the challenge. Take note of how you feel, are you sleeping better, are you waking up more positively? How's your mood been lately, more stable and balanced? How do you feel about yourself, how's your self-image changed? These are all questions I want you to ask yourself after having completed the challenge because I can promise you that you're going to be absolutely blown away by the incredible results.

What you do from here is up to you. You can continue using these tips in your diet, mixing them up and swapping them about to see what works best for you, your lifestyle etc. and keep on receiving incredible bonuses for months and months from your new approach to nutrition or you can continue to go back to your old diet, at the end of the day you've not lost out anything, if you're that desperate for a biscuit and you feel like you've missed out then you can just eat another biscuit, just realise before you do that by now, you're already more than halfway to changing your diet to help create a powerful, disease-fighting body that reflects your self-image of beauty and devotion. Good luck, and I wish you all the absolute very best in your results and success!

LAST WORDS

For all of you who have read through this far and are willing to face the challenge head-on, I want to personally congratulate you.

It takes an immense amount of focus, mental strength and willpower to do something everyone and everything in our modern society aims at us not to do – care about ourselves in a simple and easy way.

Even reading this book fully is a task that should be congratulated in itself, even if for some of you it was read in one sitting and could have been done with one eye closed, it shows how devoted and how much you desire to change when it comes to your personal health, albeit physical or mental.

My strongest and best advice I can give to anyone who is devoted, who is strong-willed and who cares more about their health than they do what others think, what others say or how others want to judge them is that you must, and I don't want to be pushy but you must, remove meat and dairy from your diet if you ever wish to be at peak health and vitality.

Yes you can achieve absolutely astonishing standards from following the 7-Day Challenge and you will reach new heights in all aspects of life but every portion of anything based around meat and dairy is always going to knock you two steps back from your progress. You cannot fight fire with fire, you cannot out-nutrition poor nutrition.

Just as you would not expect to purge a day full of chocolate, ice-cream, cake, biscuits, fizzy drinks and alcohol and expect to feel okay by eating a salad the next, you cannot expect to eat produce containing masses of pharmaceutical drug cocktails, steroids, genetically modified soy (highest oestrogen levels are found in GMO soy) and full of adrenaline from a being that has suffered and experience traumatic abuse, suffering, losses and often a hand shoved up its rear end whilst it's chained up and be able to balance it out with a little bit of kale. It simply is not possible.

I truly never wish the word 'vegan' had begun because all it does is give people an image in their mind of who they think we are, in reality, we are all the same as those who ate meat for many years (barring the occasional person born into a plant-based background), we've just come across a very unnerving, sickening and horrific truth we want to share with you.

One we don't want to be hidden from you for your own sake, for the sake of those around you and for the sake of the beings that are being harmed because you do not realise.

Since you're reading this book, you have some idea, faith and trust that I know what I'm talking about. I'm not expecting you to sit yourself down and subject yourself to all the footage shown from within the slaughter or dairy industry. In fact, I'd rather you don't for your own peace of mind unless you do truly believe your steak came from a 'happy cow', if so then you need to pop your own little bubble for your own well-being. Although to most of you, all I'm asking is that you realise one simple thing;

"You cannot consume the deadly remains of a tortured being and expect to feel lively and well, just as you cannot consume the lively remains of a thriving, nutritious plant and expect to feel unwell."

- *George Cook*

Acknowledgements

Due to fair privacy, I am going to keep the names of the following hidden, however, I want to share my immense gratitude to a few people in my life who are not only friends but are my family.

The people that have helped guide me along this journey that I had no idea how to pursue and for also inspiring me to realise that I do have the ability and the dedication to make my aspirations a reality.

To RDB, HG and MF, thank you!

About the Author

George Cook has been a health and wellness advocate for years, working with people over the country improve their state of well-being and vitality, helping people with many forms of disease and illness to live a happier, healthier and more rewarding lifestyle.

Starting off as a Personal Trainer, his talents for not only improving health states but also uplifting moods of anyone in his proximity soon showed that George had a remarkable talent. Upon finding this, his research continued throughout many areas of health and well-being including nutrition, mind and body fitness, Reiki energy healing, psychology and many broad and narrow subjects of science focused around the body, brain and the chemistry involved.

Through looking at the health of a person from the diverse array of perspective one really needs to understand the entirety of how it works, George aims to find the fundamental key ingredients to help those who are not where they want to be in life regarding their state of health.

One of his key principles is Nutrition, understanding that besides water consumption, nothing else is supposed to enter our bodies and when used in the right way, nothing else should be required.

Forthcoming Title: Faith over Fear

How would you feel if I was to tell you that your psychological suffering could all be abolished by as simple as it being your choice? No medication, no therapy, just the fact you've had enough and don't want to deal with it anymore? You'd probably think I was mad.

However what if I was to tell you that 95% of all your thoughts are programmed on repeat and that's why you are the way you are? Once again you'd think I was mad.

Psychologists today actually conclude that we have an estimate of around 65,000 thoughts in a day. Yes, 65,000 thoughts. Psychologists also conclude that anywhere up to 95% of all those thoughts are subconscious. In short, **you are running almost completely on autopilot.** *Literally, 5% of your entire life is done due to your conscious choice, the rest is on autopilot.*

With that, I'm going to tell you that that your depression, your anxiety and your psychological state right now is nothing other than just that. Patterns your mind has created. Patterns your mind continues to relay. Patterns that you can change in an instant!

This thought alone, if you're in a time of hardship may take a lot to accept, in fact, you'll likely not believe it at all because you'll feel like you've been lied to and you've suffered in a way 'for nothing' and I understand that. That is exactly how I felt after finding out the information myself after being categorised with more labels than I could count with my fingers over the time I was considered, or felt depressed, which if it helps you realise we were in the same boat, I too grew up my entire adolescence not wanting to ever wake up in the morning.

Nothing was ever changing no matter what I or anyone else tried to do, nothing. In my despair, I convinced myself like you may have very likely attempted, that I am just like this and there is no change and that's just life, after all, we're told it's not fair.

One day all of that changed, for whatever reason, I stumbled on bits of information within my research that over the course of many, many months of intense study, finally came together. I was able to leave almost a decade of life controlling and destroying depression, anxiety and paranoia behind in an instant and so were so many of my close friends who had suffered rather similarly.

This is all down to a fairly recent revelation in psychology known as neuroplasticity, which as the name denotes, our brains can be moulded. Like a child learning new tasks, at any age our brain can be moulded or shift entire belief structures and thought patterns, we're just less likely to do so as we get older.

So yes, you can try to argue with yourself why you didn't do anything about your psychological state soon, you can try to argue that you've tried everything in the books and you're also helpless, but you're not. You may not have ever possessed the knowledge previously to do anything about it but now you do. Now you no longer have to subject yourself to suffering because your minds caught up in habits because that's all it is.

There's a reason the term personality (which is also just a group of habitual thoughts in the subconscious mind) and psychological disorder is used in the realms of psychology and that's because we are literally working with a messy pattern of thoughts within the psychology. Habitual patterns that do not lead the person on a very good path in life.

You've suffered for too long, you know you have, I know you have. It's time to change. It's time to become the change. It's time to take control because no one else can ever touch your health state, but you have full control.

Through reading through the length of Faith over Fear, I promise to offer everything you need in regards to curing — yes I said the rather controversial word we're not allowed to use in modern day medicine — and removing your depression, anxiety and other psychological distress, through a full understanding of the mind, how it works, how it ended up the way it is and the information, understanding and the practical guidance to every step of the shockingly, sickeningly simple and quick journey.

To stay up to date with new releases or to find out more information about other aspects of my work then head over to:
www.facebook.com/TheVitalityGuruUK
www.instagram.com/TheVitalityGuru

For contact via email:
george@thevitalityguru.co.uk (general)
publishing@thevitalityguru.co.uk (for sales request, offers or other associated enquiries)

Printed in Poland
by Amazon Fulfillment
Poland Sp. z o.o., Wrocław